T0064512

FROM PRESSURE
TO
Potential

From Pressure
to
Potential

Renae Rollins

***

"DON'T LET THE PRESSURES IN YOUR LIFE BRING YOU DOWN. USE THAT PRESSURE TO PUSH YOU TO YOUR GREATEST POTENTIAL".

-Renae Rollins

authorHOUSE®

AuthorHouse™
1663 Liberty Drive
Bloomington, IN 47403
www.authorhouse.com
Phone: 1 (800) 839-8640

Published by AuthorHouse   08/14/2015

ISBN: 978-1-5049-2697-3 (sc)
ISBN: 978-1-5049-2696-6 (e)

Print information available on the last page.

Any people depicted in stock imagery provided by Thinkstock are models,
and such images are being used for illustrative purposes only.
Certain stock imagery © Thinkstock.

This book is printed on acid-free paper.

DEDICATION

I would like to dedicate this book to my Three wonderful
children. I allways said, God have me three reasons
to live, He gave me three reasons to push pass my
pressure and live up to my greatest potential. Reenie,
Niesha,Joshuah. I am and will allways be your greatest
example that, God can take you from nothing to
something, not just one time but every time. I love
y'all with all my heart and soul. And always remember
no matter what life brings your way "Just Dance"!

SPECIAL THANKS

———◦◦◦———

I would like to give special thanks to my Momma, the Late Claudia Mae Rollins

Thank you for birthing me, Thank you for carrying me those long 9 months, I can only imagine how hard it must have been carrying me on your own. You didn't have to go through with it. You could have easily aborted me. But you didn't. Thank you for giving me a wonderful Sister and Brother who Love's me dearly. Thank you Momma for showing me which avenues not to take. I honor you Momma because after living 51 years I can honestly say if we don't watch it life can snatch any of us into a down spiral. I get it Claudia Rollins. Rest in Peace and know I will always Love you, There isn't a day that goes by I don't think of you.

Special Thanks to the Late Johnnie Mae Crump

Thank you Grandma, for taking us in when life got hard for us. Thank you for taking that long ride to Philly to go get your Grand babies. They don't make Grandma's like you anymore. Thank you so much for showing me what a real family is supposed to be like. Thank you when you only had one bowl of grits you would share it with me. Thank you for not letting me and my cousins fight stay mad. you for the family meetings when things got out of hand. I miss you Grandma. Thank you for being the glue, that kept us together. Thank you for giving me a wonderful Auntie, and Uncles who gave us cousins that we can't count. No were not a perfect family but YES! WE ARE FAMILY!!!

Special Thanks to my Dad

I Love you Daddy, I know, you tried, you gave it your best shot. You took us along with you, You didn't leave us behind. It takes a real man to try and try and try. I must say you are a Real man. I thank you daddy for being there when we called, thank you for showing up when we needed you the most, Thank you for being a listener and never judging me. Thank you for that bowl of vanilla Ice Cream after Dinner. Thank you Daddy for that. Most of all Thank you for a wonderful Step Mom and Brother.…

FOREWORD

—◈◈◈—

Life is a montage of happenings. Some of those happens are good. Some of those happenings are bad. Some of those happenings are indifferent in their nature and have absolutely no affect on our lives. The good happenings are easiest to deal with because they are the moments in life that we enjoy most. I strongly contend that the true measure of a person cannot be tested during indifferent happenings or good happenings because those moment require very little adjustment or faith. But it's during the moments in life when we face the most difficulty that we can truly assess a person's character and integrity.

Renae Rollins knows all about difficult times and has proven to be an overcomes on every sense of the word. From childhood let downs to adulthood miscalculations, Renae has endured the worst of times, yet she has somehow found the fortitude to evolve into on the world's finest assists. The very thing that the devil design to destroy her destiny are the very things that she has allowed to shape her purpose and sharpen her vision. But to know Renae and to know her struggle and success is to know that she believes in the power that rests in her God.

As a woman of faith and obligation to serve God, this trailblazing woman has been able to turn tragedy into triumph. To have become the person she is and the entrepreneur she is has to be one of God's greatest displays of Grace, Mercy, and undeniable predestined plan of one's life. This book is going to bless you. Hearing her story is going to inspire you. Knowing that you too can overcome any obstacle is going to encourage you to be the best you can be. Life is a montage of happenings. Whether you're dealt the good, the bad, or the indifferent, play the hand you've been dealt and you'll find that in the end it was God who was strategizing the whole time and He will get the Glory out of your story.

Pastor Clarence Jackson II

PRESSURE TO POTENTIAL

Who said that dreams don't come true?

Although I grew up in what we called a "dysfunctional" family environment, I somehow had the ability to dream. As a child I had three dreams that I deeply desired. I dreamt of Hollywood, California. I talked about Hollywood so much until they gave me the nickname, *Ms. Hollywood.* And lastly, I dreamt of owning my own beauty school. Although these dreams seemed far from real at the time, inside of me I still believed that I could accomplish them.

No matter how bad your situation is and no matter what obstacles get in your way, you must have the ability to dream! You must see past your current situation and keep a burning desire to push your way through. That's what pressure to potential is about. Now, did I have a hard time achieving these childhood dreams? Yes, everything that could come up against me did. I had three bad marriages, people who I thought were friends walked out on me, and the death of my beloved mother.

But, people let me tell you **"DREAMS DO COME TRUE!"** I own a beauty salon and beauty school and at the age of forty-seven, I took my first trip to Hollywood, California and it was amazing! It was everything I dreamed it would be! San Francisco was beautiful and I got to see the Golden Gate Bridge and Alcatraz. I sat by the water and ate at "Bubba Gump's" restaurant and I even seen "The Crooked Street". As I drove from San Francisco to Hollywood, the mountains surrounded me and they had snow on them. There was palm and pine trees that sat in the front of the mountains; when the sun set it was breathtaking! My cousin and I strolled down Hollywood Boulevard and just like I imagined for days and nights; that HOLLYWOOD sign, there it was! I got to the sign and I felt like a little girl again! This might not mean much to some, but to me it meant that God truly loved me. How could a person like me accomplish her childhood dreams? I know it was nobody but GOD! *Today I can say to you to keep dreaming, keep living, never give up, don't let anything and anyone stop you and your dreams will come true.*

Pressure to Potential (P2P)

"DON'T LET THE PRESSURES IN YOUR LIFE TAKE YOU DOWN, USE THEM TO PUSH YOU TO YOUR GREATEST POTENTIAL!"

MY PRESSURE: I believe life has more to offer than what we experience when we're young. Life can deal a person a bad hand; or at least the hand can seem bad. As a young girl, I remembered my childhood seemed dark. It seemed it was dark and rainy most of the time. Momma was always coming in the house late. Daddy…well he was there in the beginning.

Talk about life being hard, Momma was drunk a lot. I remember the parties lasting all weekend long. The people would start coming on Friday night and they didn't go home until Sunday night. I remember being on the top step waiting for the people to leave.

The moment they left we hit the bottles. The liquor that was left would be ours. I just never thought it was wrong for us to hit the bottles, I mean, everyone else did.

As time went on we moved from place to place with Momma. I tell you it was **SO** cold in Philadelphia. When I was about nine years old, Marijuana was introduced. Momma would smoke her some weed and there I was hitting my first joint at nine years old. The high was good and we would laugh and smoke all day. Momma kept a lot of it.

I remember I skipped about twenty-six days from school and not realized it. When the teachers called my house, I was surprised. I had no idea that I had skipped that many days out of school. I think I was so high that I forgot to go (HA HA). But, oh, how I loved Momma. Momma was the best person, but Momma was hardly there. The only time I got to see Momma was on the bar steps. Every day I went to the bar to do Momma's hair in finger waves. Oh, how I loved to do Momma's hair.

I finally started back into high school and began to work hard to finish. As time went, Angel dust stepped on the scene. Mom said the Angel dust was going to make her as skinny as I was (I think I was about a children's size eight). Momma was always a big woman, I would say about 250 lbs. or more. Momma battled weight all her life. The parties, eating, and drinking only made her bigger. Well, the Angel dust did the trick; my brothers and sisters were home alone for weeks at a time. The next time we seen Momma, she was as little as I was. She could almost wear my dress. Momma had a friend that had lost the weight using drugs. My Momma was really gone; we had heard that Angel dust was driving people mad. I remember Momma showing me ten bags of dust. I was scared. My Momma was gone; I mean really gone crazy.

Momma finally made it home one day after a long week of being gone. She was so high. Momma opened the door. We were all sleep. It had to be in the early morning. Momma called out, *"Y'all, Mother F, get up, no one move. If ya'll don't get up I'm gonna burn ya'll asses up."*

No one would move. After a little while we began to smell smoke and someone woke up (the house was always full of people). The house was on fire. Momma had set the curtains on fire.

We all got out safe, but Momma, off to jail she went. That left us kids living alone. We were everywhere. Dad was somewhere (I don't know), but I don't remember seeing much of him. Momma eventually had a court date set.

My godmother said, *"Ya'll kids go on to school now. Your Momma got a court date on tomorrow."* She made it clear she did not want us down at the courthouse because Momma was being charged with arson. She said Momma was going to get some jail time.

By this time I was about thirteen years old. I never had been to the Philadelphia courthouse in my life. The next day I got up and headed downtown to find my Momma at the courthouse. I can remember about three inches of snow on the ground. I don't know where I got the money for the bus ride, but I had some spare change from somewhere.

As I walked through those doors I gave a person my Momma's name. They pointed to the way of the courtroom she was in. I wanted to see my Momma so bad.

There was Momma, they bought her out and I was the only one in the courtroom (I can't ever tell this story without crying). Momma's eyes were grey, as if she had no life in her. She looked at me with a little grin. The judge just looked at me. I couldn't understand what he was talking about. But the next thing you know… Momma was free to go.

I saw my Momma walking towards me. Momma had no coat, no socks, and very skimpy clothes and it was so cold outside. I gave Momma one of my gloves, and my scarf, and there we were catching the bus home. No one could believe Momma got out of jail. By this time, Momma had lost everything. All those friends were gone. She made the announcement that we were leaving for Miami. Of course, we did not want to go. All our friends were here, but Momma insisted on going.

Here we are at Grandma's house. We did fine for a while, but before long Momma would start drinking and getting high again. We were with Grandma so we were fine. By then I started feeling like I was somebody. I would say this came from God. I would start to dress up, and do my hair in many different styles. I would do my cousin's hair also.

By high school we were still partying and getting high because there was a lot dope in Grandma's house, but it was done discreetly because Grandma did not play that. One day I went to school and my guidance counselor wanted to meet with me for something. She said to me, "You are so beautiful, who did your hair like that?" I answered her that I did my hair. She told me that I should be a beautician. I thought about it and said to her, "I like doing hair, but that wouldn't be a good thing because people don't get their hair done much." She quickly responded, *"Women got their hair styled all through the First World*

War!" She made me realize that if women got their hair done in during war then it must be a good business. From there the seed was planted and I began to imagine. I told myself, *"Maybe I can be a hairstylist because oh' how I love to do hair!"*

Well, guess what? More pressure. Momma wanted to move from Grandma's house; she wanted me to stay and finish school, but I wanted to be with my siblings and Momma. So we moved to Cairo, Georgia. When we got there the drug use continued heavier this time because we would have a living room full of drugs. Momma said there was some bad marijuana going around, so she supplied us with the good stuff. Momma had been in and out of rehab and insanity hospitals. We began to party every night. I would party so hard I couldn't go to school. Momma would be out all night.

One day my big sister said, *"You going to school today! If you can party all week, then you can go to school."* She had just finished twelfth grade. She would nag me until I got up out the bed *(thank you, sis, I love you)*. I had six months to go in order to finish high school and it was a struggle, but I knew deep down inside that if I didn't finish high school then I would never finish anything. Wow! I did it; somehow I made it. I believe God had his hands on us. I remember as a young girl in Philly that I use to see demons a lot. I could never sleep alone. Momma would send me to the Jehovah's Witnesses' house to let them pray the demons out. I guess it worked. I know one thing; by fourteen years old I was introduced to Islam, and other religions.

When I graduated from high school I had to get back to Philadelphia. I wanted to see my friends again. I had a plane ticket and there I went, only to find out that those people who I thought were friends were now cold and dirty. I was living from house to house with people I thought I knew. Eventually, I worked to get my own apartment.

I worked, and then I heard about a beauty school downtown. I signed myself up. Although I had financial aid, I still had to pay for school, so I was a maid part time and worked at Gino's fast food, going to beauty school at night. Talk about pressure! I would carry my cosmetology book everywhere I went. I knew all the odds were against me. I felt like it was just God and I. Even though I didn't know God, I felt God knew me *(living with those demons, and going to get prayed for every week helped)*.

In beauty school, the director of the school was Ms. Sylvia. She must have been the most fly lady I had ever seen. Her hair stayed neat as a whistle, every strand in place. My teacher was so fierce, and her make-up would be flawless. I wanted to be like her.

"Young people, although everything and everyone in your surroundings could be negative; step outside your world, and do something positive! God will put examples in your path so that you can begin to learn about the positive side of you."

Beauty school caused me to lighten up! Then I heard my great grandmother had died. I was almost finished with the program. I made the decision to move back to Miami. I went in to talk to my director, who I was fond of. She said, *"I see you are transferring to the Wilfred Academy in Miami. Well, I hope to visit you in your salon down there."* I looked at her and said, *"You think I will one day own my own salon?"* Looking at me straight in the eye, she replied, *"I have no doubt you will one day own a salon."*

I held on to those words forever. I moved to Florida, and of course I never got into beauty school. Instead, I got married at the age of twenty-one. I was so good at doing hair by then, I had brought hairstyles from Philly and New York; and I must say I was good at what I did.

I was able to bootleg in a salon, but eventually the owner let the salon go. I was out of work and lived with an aunt. I had not seen Momma for a long time. She may have even been in jail. Somehow, God allowed a lady to call me. She was opening up a new salon and she needed someone to run it while she gave her two weeks notice. I was pretty well known by then. I ran her shop at the age of eighteen until she was able to come over.

People would come from everywhere. I had people lined up out the door. One day, the word got out that I wasn't licensed. I was making a thousand dollars a week. So, of course I was pushed to finish beauty school. I only needed three hundred hours. I finished and was headed to State Board. WOW! What would I have done without the pressure? Of course, I passed. I knew the book back and forth, and I wanted it bad.

Things went well for me. I bought a car, but I married the wrong man. Hell is what it was. We were the best couple (In others eyes). I got introduced to Jesus. I would hear Grandma praying to him all the time. But I thought she was going through the motions. Well, after being with an addict and Drug dealer, I found that man my Grandmother used to call on. I found peace, love, and joy in him. I would pray for the Lord to be my Momma and my Daddy.

Momma came from somewhere, I don't know where, and this time she was a full-fledged crack addict. I moved Momma into my *house (here I go again trying to save Momma)*. She did well for a while. We would cook food and go take it to the homeless shelter. My Momma and I were good Christians.

I was happy Momma was trying hard. One day Momma didn't show up to feed the hungry. The next thing I knew Momma started smoking crack in the house. I would find little burnt aluminum foil on the back steps.

I was determined by now that I was going to live a positive life, a life for Jesus. I knew how it was my only way out. I would carry my Bible like I carried my Cosmetology book. I needed out! I felt trapped. I would still do hair! It was my life, and I was good at it.

MARRYING THE WRONG MAN

Different things happened during my first marriage. That day, I planned my escape.

I was determined at this point to get out. I hated to leave my home and my first business, but I knew if I didn't get out I would die. I had my three-year-old daughter, God, my hot curlers and scissors. I believed that I could do all things through Christ. I knew I was more than a Conqueror through Christ Jesus; I was a "Jesus freak".

My ex-husband would come sit on the church grounds and when I got out of church he would be sitting on the car with his beer waiting for me. Disappointed by Momma once again.

One night, about one o' clock in the morning; we snuck out on a bicycle. I had my salon by then, but I must say it was nothing like I thought it would be (marrying the wrong person, that is). I still dreamed, and I still believed that God was with me.

I thought about all the hell I had been through all of my life, and how God had helped me to survive. I knew in my innermost being that he would bring me out.

ON THE RUN AGAIN

I was on the run again with my baby. I was twenty-four years old and still running. Looks as though my dreams were shattered. However, I still had hope. With the Word engraved in my spirit I went to my beauty shop, grabbed my hot curlers and scissors, left everything else, and left the bike at my Grandma's house. I had $121. It was enough for a one-way ticket to Havana, Florida where my big sister lived.

WOMEN: YOU CAN GET OUT. My baby and I got out alive. We were broke, but we were alive.

MY GIFT MADE ROOM
FOR ME (MY Potential)

Hair was what I knew. So, that's what I did. I had no time to look for a job. I had my skills and they worked for me. Whatever you do in life, work your gift! We all have them. By the time I got to Havana with my big sister,

I felt safe. It was a long time before I got into another church. Two girls knew I was good with hair because I would do my sister's hair when she came to Miami. I styled those two ladies and the rest was history. People would come from all over to get their hair done in the singlewide trailer a sheriff in Havana fixed up especially for me to live. On one side I had my bed bathroom and shower, and do hair on the other side. I had a regular sitting chair to style hair and a beach chair to shampoo client's hair.

God was with me. But I had left him, the parties began and I was making good money. I was mocking what I had seen all my life. No one in town was doing the styles I would do. I named the place, Renae's Creations. I created hairstyles and clothes for girls to model. I did fashion shows in all the clubs, and before I even realized it, I had totally backslid.

If I were to be honest, even though God had never left me and we had gotten out, I felt the devil had won, because I had lost everything. Momma didn't stay off those drugs, and the man I married was crazy. I couldn't see the blessings because I was focused on my failures. Although I was blessed, I was alive and had come to a town with nothing. I never had to look for a job. My baby and I never missed a meal. My stepmother (I love her so much) sent money for us to buy clothes.

The customers continued to come, and before long I had my own acreage of land on a main highway and had moved the shop to a building with real shampoo chairs and shampoo sinks. I didn't realize God still had me. I began to recognize my behavior, because the behavior started looking similar to our childhood days. I remember I would always hear the words, *"You're going to be something in life."*

I began to switch my strategy to get my styles out in the community. I began to give fashion shows at the high school, and community centers, where there was no drinking involved, and before I knew it God was calling me back to his church (I love you, Jesus). I owned a number of houses by this time. The cars I wanted, I bought. My ex-husband came down to try to get me to go back, but it was too late.

Here comes Momma again. She needed so much help. Momma had ruined her life, and once again I reached out to help her. But Momma's mind was bad by now. People would tell me they had seen my Momma under bridges. I would go to those bridges and look for her. I longed for her to be a good Momma, but I realized that I had to let her go. Things were going well for me. I was married for the second time *(I know it was for protection; my ex kept coming to try to get me to move back with him)*. This man was younger, I was a mature businesswoman by then, but I needed protection, so I married him.

LIVING LIFE: GOD'S WAY

I made a 100% change in my life at this point. I decided to throw myself into the one and only mother and father I knew, and that was God. God had become my parents again; He was my real savior and protection. I grabbed my Bible and began to live the life I was predestined to live. I knew when all else failed; He was my comforter, my redeemer. I knew I could hide myself in Him. He was my strength.

I just had a feeling in my gut that I couldn't live my life without Jesus. I saw so many of the people I partied with never giving church or God any thought. But somewhere inside of me there was always a pull toward something different. I began to separate myself from the friends I was running with. I stopped buying liquor. After that I have not seen or heard from those friends anymore.

I began going to the neighborhood church, and I felt like a fish that had finally found its tank again. I began to flourish in God. I was there for a while; God called me to preach, I had a word in my spirit, I woke up that Sunday morning, I prayed and pondered with it. I said to God, *"Are you sure you want me to carry your word?"*

God said yes. I made an appointment with my pastor, and he said, *"WOW!"* a word he always used. He said he just had a dream. He said he thought it was a man. He confirmed that God had called me, because He had already showed him a minister being birth in his ministry *(I was the first one)*.

Soon after that God birthed a dance ministry in me. Oh, how I always loved to dance. I would dance all night at the club. One time in school we had an assembly and I was in middle school. I was up dancing and I fell asleep dancing! It was as if I went into a trance, someone shook me, and told me the music had stopped, but I tell you the music was still playing somehow in my mind.

God said to me that I could dance for Him. I began to use my gifts in the church. The dance ministry would help a lot of children come off the streets. It gave me a chance to connect with young people and help them with their issues in their teen years. Now, I'm walking in my divine purpose.

I loved the teenagers, I think because as a teenager; I struggled so hard. I did not have the affirmation of a father, but I did have a Momma on drugs, along with all of the identity and self-esteem issues that teenagers go through.

I will testify forever that because my guidance counselor told me that I was a hairdresser that she woke something up in me. I knew that I could do hair; I knew that I loved to look pretty all the time, but what I didn't know is who I was or what I was to become. She put a name on it: Madame C.J. Walker. She became my icon and I began to learn and study about her being the first black millionaire, she made it by the very talent that God had given me (Hallelujah).

See, I believe our teenagers need life spoken into them. They get into a lot, and trouble would not be an option if someone gave them the ability to dream. I thought, *"WOW, you mean little ole' me can be a hairstylist... You mean I can make money doing something I love?"* That was a revelation, and let me tell you something, that was over thirty years ago and I still remember the outfit I wore, the way I had my hair, and as a matter of fact I can see myself where I was standing in her office in Miami, Florida at Miami Jackson High School.

God gave me the gift to minister to teens and young women, about the pressures in life. The circumstances during my childhood would now become my ministry. My pain became someone else's breakthrough. *"Thank you Jesus!"* (Excuse me I have to take a praise break).

This is why I say: let the pressure in life push you. I love that saying, "When the going gets tough, the tough got to get doing." You'll notice I said "doing", not "going", because some people run from their problems.

But, as someone said, when life serves us lemons we need to make lemonade. This is my message to the great people we call teenagers and young adults. We need to label them as great, not judge them by what we see, but seeing far beyond their actions now. Someone once told me, we have to begin with the end in mind, see the end results not what you see now. I believe that you have to be gifted to understand this.

By this time I would have teen groups, teen programs, and coach young women into their destiny. I began to write programs that were geared especially to help teen girls to abstain from destructive behavior. Needless to say I am henceforth walking in my purpose.

Soon after God would send me out to a ministry that was geared to deal with teenagers just like myself, who were in drug and alcohol abusing homes. We would go to the streets and get women who were addicted; most of these women were just like Momma, who had kids they were leaving home with no guidance. My heart would melt, because that was what I had been through.

In the meetings with those women we had twice a week, I would literally cry. The one thing God allowed me to learn in those groups was that drug addiction is a disease. All the while I yearned for Momma to get off the drugs, now I can see that she couldn't because she was sick, the drugs were her God. Those women would cry and talk about how the crack would call them in their dreams. We would see women that had been on it for forty years. But I also saw women who had been clean and sober for over twenty years.

Through this ministry I could see hope for Momma. I began to have compassion for her. I now understood why Momma couldn't just stop. Of course, I was on the journey to go find Momma again to get her into the program, and I did. Momma stayed clean for two years, the longest I had ever seen her clean. We didn't see eye to eye sometimes. I think I still may have been a little bitter, and I know by her being with me all the time we would go at it every now and then. But, I was just happy Momma was clean and sober.

Two years later Momma hit the streets. But I kept on in my purpose. I was not going to let Momma get me off my focus. God had given me the strength to continue to minister to teenagers and their parents. I felt like I was the teenagers' voice. I would tell the mothers how I felt not having my Momma, and these women would listen to me. Some stayed off drugs, but some were just like Momma, answering yes to the drug call.

I think about how I could have ended up strung out and addicted. I tried to smoke the weed and drink the alcohol, but it would never stick. Somewhere inside I knew I did not want to end up like Momma.

God had shown me who I was. God had affirmed me. He said I was an entrepreneur. He said I was a hairstylist, a business owner, and a Minister of the Gospel. *(Praise Him)*

Bringing Momma Home for the Last Time

After using drugs most her life, Momma finally said she was tired and ready to come in. She lived clean and sober with my sister. After about six months Momma began to have seizures. These seizures would eventually leave her bed ridden. Momma stayed in a nursing home for a year. Then God told me to bring momma to my house. Without hesitance I did. Momma lived with me 3 years, my sister, brother and I would see about her. I signed her up with organizations to help take care of her and things were going great. We had to do everything for momma, but I was glad to have momma home. Three years later Momma lost her "Ability to Strive". She wanted to die. Being bed ridden took its toll. I was thankful for the time we spent together.

After having another seizure, we took Momma off of all the medications and we decided to let her go if that is what God wanted. As they rolled she back into the house she looked up at me after being sleep for four days and said, *"Renae I'm, glad to be home"*. Momma died seven days later. Momma was leaving us for the last time, Wow! That was a big lost but the time we spent in that house together was a kiss from heaven. I can truly say I love my momma and my momma truly loved me.

It doesn't matter what Momma did or didn't do, she was still my Momma! She's not going to do everything right because there is no manual for her. She just does the best that she can, but remember this, no one can ever take her place, no one can ever fill the void that momma filled! God makes the loss of a mother easier to deal with, but at the end of the day, a child still longs for their mother. I thank God for giving me that time with Momma.

Momma's Gone

I wouldn't have had it any other way because momma was with me when she took her last breath. Momma was sick and bed ridden for four long years. She spent three of the four years at home with me. We would laugh so much and although she couldn't get up, I would put on some old school music and we would dance and pop our fingers. We would put praise music on and shout and praise to God, and we read the Bible together. Every morning when I got dressed for work I would go to her room, and she would say

"Oh you so pretty, if I was pretty as you…"
I tell you I enjoyed my momma y'all. God turned a bad situation into my blessing. I not only realized how much I loved my Momma, more importantly how much Momma loved me. The love I had yearned for, through my childhood, God allowed me to have it. I didn't have to worry about momma anymore because every time I got home she was laying in that bed waiting for me to get there. When I brought Momma home for the last time my brother and the nurse stayed with her while I went to work.

Then of course we had our bad days when Momma would cuss everybody out and tell us all where to go, but that was okay, because she would cry and apologize later. She held on like a champ and would always threaten to get up and beat the kids. I thank God, that for every bad day, we would have two or three good days. Momma passed on. I looked at what the Doctor wrote on my Momma's Death Certificate for cause of death. He wrote "Lost of Ability to Thrive". I thought, WOW,

I began to pray, "Lord please don't let me lose my ability to thrive." You see, life will suck you dry, if we don't be careful. We will allow people, and things to somehow get us off focus of what our real life purpose is. We began to look at what we don't have, or what we can't do, instead of looking at the possibilities of getting up, get going, looking at the possibilities of conquering that thing that trying to conquer us. That death certificate didn't say, my Momma died from a heart attack, cancer or even from the seizures she had. It didn't say she died from abusing drugs all of her adult life. It says, "She lost her ability to thrive", (Her ability to fight back). *NEVER* lose your ability to take life by the neck and rip it off. LISTEN; There is always going to be a fight!! When you wake up in the morning the Devil needs to be shaking in his knees. LISTEN; THE FIGHT IS FIXED: WE WIN IN THE END, THROUGH JESUS CHRIST: BUT YOU MUST NEVER GIVE UP. DON'T LOSE YOUR ABILITY TO THRIVE. This is my word from the Lord.

I Am My Mother's Daughter

My uncles would tell me how my momma used to love to dance and she loved people, especially her family. Her cousins told me how before life took a grip out of her, she was so strong, pretty and tenacious, and didn't take junk from anyone. Her favorite color was red and my favorite color is red. Although, in my younger days I saw momma destroy her life with the drugs and alcohol, and I was determined not to repeat that curse. Now that I am older and Momma's gone, I realize how much alike my momma and I really am. I got this revelation one day when I thought about how I love to dance (I mean I could dance all night), I love making people laugh, and I love my family! My Momma and I also love to dress. She had so many clothes and shoes and oh how I loved her shoes when I was little. I suddenly realize how much I am *"my mother's daughter"*.

As I study my momma's life I realize that momma was a good momma, but when I got around nine or ten years old, life took a bite out of momma. She fell and couldn't bounce back from it. The people she trusted the most used momma. The partying became more important than the family. She had lost her high school sweetheart, never to get him back. I realize those things happen to all of us. This happened to me! After having kids of my own, a few bad marriages, and people turning their backs on me; I learned from momma not to lean and depend on people because I saw what it did to her. I fell too, but I fell on the Rock, the rock of Christ Jesus, *"where the gates of hell could not prevail against me"*. I fell on the Rock that I would hear grandmother praying to for hours in that bathroom, she'd be screaming Jesus name.

I refused to let life get the best of me. I refused to be taken down by the curses of our generation, NO it stops here! I have fought a good fight and I will continue fighting till the day I die. I believe when the Bible says, *"I am* the head and not the tail, that I am above and not beneath, and that I can do all things through Christ who strengthens me."

For those who are reading this book, just remember that you too have to keep the faith, you have to run your race, you have to know that you are not a product of your environment, and that you have the power within you to change your environment! It's not how you start but it's how you finish, and you must finish strong, you must Dream and "DREAM BIG!" YES, I AM MY MOTHER'S DAUGHTER, BUT MORE IMPORTANT. I AM A CHILD OF THE TRUE AND RESURRECTED JESUS, THE CHRIST.

Conclusion

—◦◦◦—

I am a Mother of three, a Minister of the Gospel a business owner, a home owner, entrepreneur, counselor, educator, actor, an inventor, a college graduate, an Insurance Agent an author, A fully Accredited Beauty school owner, and the list will continue. And, I am living my dreams, and I won't stop, I won't ever stop: TO THE TEENAGER OR YOUNG ADULT THAT IS READING THIS BOOK YOU CAN DO IT. YOU CAN BE EVERYTHING YOUR HEART DESIRES IF YOU DON'T QUIT, IF YOU LET YOUR PRESSURE, YES EVEN THAT THING YOU ARE IN RIGHT NOW. LET IT PUSH OUT YOUR GREATEST POTENTIAL. THEY COUNTED ME OUT, SAID I WAS GONNA BE A NOTHING AND NOBODY, BUT GOD COUNTED ME IN AND SAID THE DEVIL IS A LIAR. JESUS DIED SO I CAN LIVE, AND THROUGH HIM I CAN DO ALL THINGS. (THANK YOU JESUS).

"It takes hard work but every childhood dream
I had. I'm living them. From becoming a
hairstylist to owning my own Beauty School,
then writing a book about it "Live your Dreams".

ABOUT THE AUTHOR

Renae Rollins has more than 36 years of experience in the Hair and Beauty Industry. Renae Rollins has owned Salons in the Miami and North Florida areas. Among being a licensed stylist, Renae also received her college degree in Psychology and is a registered Ordained Minister for 15 years; serving in various capacities throughout the community. In 2004, Renae opened World Class Academy of Beauty, becoming a National accredited institution educating and licensing students in the field of cosmetology, Barbering, Nails and Skin. In 2006 Renae Rollins Invented the "My baby Shoulder Holder Pillow" (designed for mothers to carry their Babies on their shoulders). Renae Rollins served 12 years with Mothers In Crisis (Organization helping women and their children get off Drugs and Alcohol) also served as Vice President of the Organization. Renae Rollins developed and founded a Teen group T.A.T.S (Teens

Against Teen Sex and drugs). Renae Rollins also establish The House of Restoration which house Drug and Alcohol abused women which was instituted at Mothers in Crisis. Renae Rollins is still dedicated to helping Teens overcome obsatacles. Renae Rollins has worked as a volunteer with "LOOK GOOD,FEEL BETTER" which help taught women with Cancer how to wear, style wigs, and scarves and Make up when going through with losing their Hair. Renae Rollins still today working on her passion of helping Teens she is now developing a future program Her" Young Entrepreneurship Program" Which is designed to link Teens and Local Businesses together to teach teens how to start and run their own Businesses. Her P2P (Pressure to Potential) Program is a Life Coach Program for Teens and Young Adults. To help Coach Them from Pressure to their Greatest Potential.

To Book speaking Engagements Please feel free to call.

Renae Rollins can be reach at (850)980-5936 or WorldClass Academy of Beauty (850)580-7799

FaceBook WorldClass Academy of Beauty or Renae Rollins

Email: tatstats3@aol.com

"THERE'S A GOD IN YOU THAT'S
DRIVING YOU. TAKE YOUR HANDS OFF
THE WHEEL AND LET HIM DRIVE"

"EVERYTHING I'VE DONE IN
LIFE, I DID IT BROKE". I HAD TO
TRUST GOD, I DID IT BY FAITH.

"DREAM BIG"

WHEN LIFE SEEMS TO GET YOU
DOWN AND YOU CAN'T SEEM TO
GET THINGS IN PLACE, "DANCE".

Renae Rollins,
Motivational speaker: Entrepreneur, Spiritual Counselor Teen and Young adult coach: Facebook Renae Rollins. Face Book WorldClassAcademy of Beauty.

The "Fear of Fifty"

Fifty is fastly approaching, can't believe in two months I will be a half of 100. So many uncertainties so many unanswered questions. I have accomplished so much. But yet I have so many new inspirations I haven't accomplished. I feel that I want to change some things in my life but yet I love my life the way it is. I have a darling son, two beautiful young women(my daughters) who is now living out their own lives, and a wonderful man that I will soon call my husband and he will soon call me wife. Family and friends who love me dearly."

"Fearing Fifty"

Look what all The Lord has done, why do I fear. Am I fearing the unknown? the uncertain? Who knows? So many of my friends and even my sister, has already turned fifty, they seemed to be doing Fifty well. What is it with me? What does Fifty hold for ME, that's different from forty or forty five? If anything different. See, although I love my life. I'm that person that thrive off of change, I'm always searching for better in my life, I need different. sometimes to often. Lord please help me make sound choices. Order my steps Lord..

Taking Chances....
Where do we go from here?I have these questions lingering in my mind. I want to be everything I was born to be. I want to Die Empty! I want to do everything I was born to do.

Fifty
What does Fifty hold:
Menopause,mood swings, aching bones, hysterectomies, lumps and bumps and more bruises, blue skies, cold nights and sunny days and rose petals. Who knows, what it holds for me. Only God knows.
I am going to fight this Fear of Fifty. It's as if I can't wait, I'm anxious, it's exciting but yet scary. Fifty begins the next half of my life and as it is said in the Bible "The Half Has not Been Told".

Yes that's it. Exciting but Fearful, my Flesh is waring against my Spirit. The best of times and the worst of times all at the same time. My emotions are running rapid right now, but my My mind is made up. I am going to follow Jesus. Because I don't believe he's brought me this far to leave me. We Shall Win in the end, as it it is said in the Word of God "The race is not given to the Swift nor the Battle to the Strong, But to the one that endureth till the end. The Bible also reminds me that. "Though we been tried in the fire, We shall come forth as pure Gold". So I have learned to Fight the Good Fight. The Fight that's already been Fixed.

Remember, all of you that is fastly approaching Fifty. We WIN!!!

4:45am. Reflections.. I love you Lord. Thanks for letting me share.

Special Thanks to all my Clients. You were never just Clients you are and will always be my Friends, my Prayer Warriors and my Family. You know who you are. You were sent by God. Without you, there would be no WorldClass, YOU made me better. You started out with me when I was Renae's Creations. You hung in there with me and cultivated me, and Believed in me. I believe I am the person I am today because of you. I can't throw out names in the fear of forgetting someone. So here's a big "Thank You" to all of you. May God continue to Richly Bless you all.

My Baby Shoulder Holder Pillow

Printed in the United States
By Bookmasters